MW01712599

THE LITTLE PERSIAN *Cat Book*

ELIZABETH MARTYN
DAVID TAYLOR

RAINCOAST BOOKS
VANCOUVER

A DORLING KINDERSLEY BOOK

PROJECT EDITOR Candida Ross-Macdonald

DESIGNER Camilla Fox

MANAGING EDITOR Krystyna Mayer

MANAGING ART EDITOR Derek Coombes

PRODUCTION Lauren Britton

First Canadian Edition 1993
10 9 8 7 6 5 4 3 2 1

Raincoast Books, 112 East 3rd Avenue,
Vancouver, British Columbia V5T 1C8

Copyright © 1993 Dorling Kindersley Limited, London
Text copyright © 1993 Elizabeth Martyn and David Taylor

All rights reserved under International and Pan-American Copyright Conventions. Published and distributed in Canada by Raincoast Book Distribution. First published in Great Britain by Dorling Kindersley Limited, London. No part of this publication may be reproduced, stored in a retrieval system, or transmitted in any form or by any means, electronic, mechanical, photocopying, recording, or otherwise, without the prior written permission of the copyright owner.

ISBN 1-895714-17-6
CIP Record available. Canadiana Control No. C93-091254-3

Reproduced by Colourscan, Singapore
Printed and bound in Hong Kong by Imago

CONTENTS

LUXURIOUS *Cat*

How the opulent Persian found its way from the East to Europe and America, and won its many admirers.

Persian Origins

European explorers brought exotic felines home, and the cats have grown in popularity ever since.

The origins of these opulent cats are obscure. All domestic cats in Europe were originally shorthairs, and longhaired cats did not appear until the 16th century. But from where?

From Russia, with Love
According to one theory, longhaired cats developed in cold lands – they are still more common in Russia than in Turkey or Iran – and came to the West through Asia Minor. Another view is that they are native to Central Asia, and descended from the longhaired Manul or Pallas Cat, the native wild cat of Afghanistan and Iran.

Pietro della Valle, an Italian explorer, brought longhaired cats back from his eastern travels in 1550, and a French achaeologist, Nicolas Fabri de Peinix, imported more in the 18th century. The cats spread from France, and in Britain were called French cats.

Going West
It is possible that these first longhairs to reach Europe were white Angoras from Turkey, once kept as pets in the harems of Constantinople. The "Persian" cat we know was developed in Britain from cats brought over from Turkey or Persia in the late 19th century.

Left: Le chat Persan *makes an appearance in French advertising*
Right: Persian cat at the feast
Below: The perfect Victorian cat

When the cat appeared in America, a separate way of classifying its different types developed. In Britain, the cats are officially called Longhairs, and each color is treated as a separate breed, while in America the cats are treated as one breed, the Persian, and the colors are treated as varieties.

Hall of Feline Fame

Persian cats have enjoyed the patronage of the great, the good, and the not-so-good.

The late-19th-century rise to popularity of the Persian cat was due in part to the good looks and affable personality characteristic of the breed. The cats also held a Royal seal of approval from Queen Victoria, the century's great monarch and matriarch. Her Majesty kept no fewer than three Persian cats.

The Lady with the Cat

Another famous 19th-century lady favored Persian cats as her companions. Florence Nightingale – nurse, pioneer of hospital reform, and humanitarian heroine of the Crimean War – was a most passionate admirer of Persian cats. She owned around 60 during her life, naming some of them after great statesmen of the age including Gladstone, Disraeli, and Bismarck.

On a far less virtuous note, the French statesman and cardinal, Richelieu, is reputed to have signed death warrants with one hand, while idly stroking his black Persian cat, Lucifer, with the other. The Bond villain Blofeld was also a Persian cat fan, appearing with Solomon, a sparkling white Chinchilla.

Arty Cats

Many writers and artists have been drawn to the charm of the Persian cat. Novelist Raymond

Left: Colette and constant companion
Above: Rebecca West, an English writer with a Persian pet
Right: Nurse Florence Nightingale had an iron will, but a soft spot for her Persians

Chandler gained inspiration from the constant company of his black Persian, Taki. French writer Colette adored cats, even playing one on stage in *La Chatte Amoreuse*. Her first work to be published under her own name took the form of conversations between her Angora, Kiki la Doucette, and her dog. Cats featured in many of her works, both fictional and autobiographical. Colette's compatriot, Jean Cocteau, owned a Blue Persian that mated with his Siamese. This unlikely parental partnership produced one particularly adorable grandchild, a fluffy black kitten described by Cocteau as resembling "a kind of black semi-colon."

GALLERY OF *Cats*

A line-up of sumptuous cats with coats you'll long to stroke.

FELINE FEATURES

Persian and breeds derived from them have snub faces, with round eyes that are usually green, gold, or copper. Their close neighbors, Angoras and Turkish Vans, have longer faces, but the same regal aspect.

ANGORA
Cinnamon

HIMALAYAN
Seal Point

TURKISH VAN
Auburn and white

TIFFANY
Smoke

Brown Tabby Persian

Smoke Persian

Red Self Persian

Chinchilla

Ragdoll
Seal Bi-color

Non-pedigree Longhair

Persian Coat Colors

A Persian cat's luxurious coat has a soft undercoat for warmth and a topcoat of longer guard hairs. The silky fur of Angoras and Turkish Vans lacks the undercoat. Persians and Angoras come in every feline shade, from self colors to tortoiseshells, and the Turkish Van is appearing in more colors as it grows in popularity.

Tortoiseshell Persian
Chocolate

Tortie and White Persian

Bi-color Persian
Chocolate and White

Angora
Cream

Brown Tabby
Persian

Red Cameo
Shaded Persian

Tortoiseshell
Persian
Smoke

Golden Persian

Smoke Persian

Himalayan

Chocolate
Persian

Bi-color Persian
Red and white

Blue-cream
Persian

BLUE PERSIAN

Careful breeding has ensured that the Blue Persian is now considered the ultimate of the type, and it is often used in breeding to improve other varieties. Known in Persia from the 16th century, it has also been suggested that the breed originated in China, Afghanistan, or Russia, and there is evidence that it was known in India and Renaissance Italy. The Blue first won fame in Britain in the late 19th century, and its admirers formed the Blue Persian Society in 1901 with Royal Patronage.

CATERISTICS

Thoroughly enjoys family life

Likes being the center of attention

Intelligent and even-tempered

FLUFF BALL

A snub little face in a powder puff of fur shows the typical features of the type. The ears are small and delicate, with round tips and tufts of fur in front. The eyes are rounded, and may be copper or orange.

FADE AWAY

Blue kittens often have noticeable tabby markings at birth, which fade in time to give an all-over blue. It is impossible to tell what the coat will finally look like, as the kittens with the strongest markings often – but not always – grow up with the purest coats. Baby Blues have forget-me-not eyes, which transform into those golden spheres over the first few months of life.

BLACK BEGINNINGS

The soft, smoky gray of the luxuriant coat that swathes the Blue from head to paw is a genetic dilution of black, probably originally produced by breeding a White Persian with a black mate.

WHITE PERSIAN

A real glamor-puss with an irresistibly silky coat, the White Persian is undoubtedly a connoisseur's cat. Its ancestry can be traced back to the white Angora, which was first introduced into Europe from Turkey in the 16th century. Three centuries later, the Victorians had the bright idea of crossing the Angora with the Persian, and the result was this stunning cat with its regal expression and peace-loving personality.

LUSCIOUS CREAM

Cream Persians were the result of breeding Blues or Tortoiseshells with Reds.

Color Mix

With its quirky looks, the Odd-eyed White has a special kind of charm. Unfortunately, this type may suffer from deafness on its blue-eyed side. Newborns have blue eyes, one turning deep orange as the kitten grows up.

Glowing Eyes

Orange-eyed Whites are more often seen than the Blue-eyed variety, because they tend to have larger litters, and it is difficult to breed a blue-eyed cat true to the pedigree standards. Together with their first-class coats, the Orange-eyed Whites have the snub faces that are desirable in prizewinners.

Cateristics

No more delicate than other types, despite its fragile appearance

Particularly suited to indoor life

Fastidious and always well groomed

Black Persian

One of the first longhaired cats to be developed in Europe, the Black Persian originally resembled the Angora, with a long nose and large ears. These characteristics have now been bred out, and the Black Persian has been awarded Cat of the Year a record-breaking three times in the United States. Perfect specimens are few and far between, because of the difficulty in achieving a coat that is totally black; there must be no white hairs, nor any hint of rust, gray, or tabby. The ideal coat is hardly ever found in young cats, but develops as the cat matures and may fade again in old age.

Pert Puss

That snubbed face sports a smart set of long whiskers. The Black Persian becomes alert and high-spirited when its curiosity is aroused.

Sun and Shade

Care and attention are needed to keep the black coat in top condition. Show cats should be kept out of the wet to avoid a brownish tinge. Sunbathing is also banned, because intense light can bleach the coat.

CATERISTICS

A warm and affectionate nature

Sometimes wary of strangers

Can be quite lively and bouncy

BLACK AND BLUE

If two Black Persians are mated they will produce black offspring, but the type is improved by cross-breeding with either Blues or Whites.

Chinchilla

A cat with real sparkle, the Chinchilla is the result of cross-breeding between colors including the Smoke and the Silver Tabby. Originally the breed was darker, but since its first appearance in the 1890s it has been refined to the delicate creature recognized today. The coat is white, but some hairs are tipped with black. Unusually for a Persian, the Chinchilla's eyes are emerald- or blue-green, made unforgettable by their dark rims.

Shimmer and Shine
The tips of some of the guard hairs are lightly colored, producing a subtle shimmer.

SILVER NAMESAKE

The Chinchilla takes its name from a rodent native to South America. The rodent Chinchilla is bred for its soft coat, which is dark underneath and tipped with white to give an overall effect of silvery-gray. In the feline Chinchilla the shades of the coat are reversed, to give a color that is not so much the gray of its namesake as white-with-a-hint-of-a-glint.

CATERISTICS

Less passive than other Persian breeds

Requires punctilious grooming to look its best

Kittens may be born striped

TRUE COLORS

Early Chinchillas had hazel eyes. Blue-eyed White Persians were added to the mix, and the result was the hypnotic green or blue-green we see today.

Red Self Persian

To produce a Red Self whose coat shows no trace of tabby markings is a real challenge to breeders. Although their luxuriant fur can be an effective disguise, many have evidence of their tabby origins showing through somewhere. Faint spots or stripes appear most commonly on the face, legs, or tail. Kittens are often born with tabby markings, which may or may not disappear when they reach maturity. The breed has been known in Britain since 1880, when it was called the Orange, and has regained popularity after becoming scarce in the 1940s.

Tortie Charmer
Red, mottled with cream and black, gives this rich Tortoiseshell coat. This is a female-only breed, and kittens are prized for their rarity.

Cateristics

Silky, strokable fur

Well mannered and sedate; an excellent domestic pet

Unusual to see a coat of uniform red

Matching Accessories

To blend with the overall color scheme, even the paws and the nose should be red. Lips and chin likewise should be red, rather than the black seen in other varieties.

Orange Orbs

Copper-colored eyes should be large, shining, and saucer-like. The face is rounded, with luxuriant whiskers and fluffy ear tufts.

LILAC PERSIAN

An artificial color, produced by strict selective breeding, the Lilac is still rare. Self-color kittens occasionally appeared in Himalayan litters, from which breeders produced the Chocolate coat. Subsequently, by introducing Blue genes into the recipe, they created these most beautiful cats with coats of pinkish gray or pale lavender. Breeding must still be carefully monitored to produce the best possible coat colors.

REGAL RUFF

The coat is full and fluffy, with a sumptuous frill draped over the chest. The fur is soft and silken, and of course requires meticulous daily grooming to keep it in top condition and free from tangles. The delicious, pinky gray color remains very elusive.

CATERISTICS

Has a streak of Siamese high spirits

Coat has the same color from root to tip

The paw pads and nose are a matching pink

BODYWORK

In shape and build the Lilac is typical of all Persians, with a solid, stocky body, bushy tail, and short legs.

LAVENDER LAD

Producing the eye-smacking lavender coat proved a headache in the early days. It was some years before a stable color allowed a show standard to be approved. Even now the color is unusual, and kittens tend to be expensive and hard to come by.

Turkish Van

Cat breeders never stop looking for unusual felines, even when on holiday. The Turkish Van was spotted in the 1950s by a British breeder on holiday near Lake Van in southeastern Turkey. The cat had been a common domestic pet in this isolated region for many centuries. A pair was brought back to England; they were found to breed true, all kittens carrying the same markings as their parents. And there's no mistaking the markings of the Turkish Van, with its chalky white coat and amber face and tail. The breed has another unforgettable characteristic: it loves to play with water and takes a dip at any opportunity, hence its popular name, the Turkish Swimming Cat. One advantage of this odd quirk is that the cat will willingly take a bath if its white coat should get grubby.

New Look

The Turkish Van – which is now bred in other colors, like this tortie-and-white – needs only light daily combing to keep it sleek and silky.

CATERISTICS

A competent swimmer that delights in water

Lively, loving, and very clever

Easy to groom

SACRED SYMBOL

Legend has it that the white mark on the Turkish Van's forehead is the thumbprint of Allah.

ODDITY

Most Turkish Vans have amber eyes, but kittens with one blue and one amber eye do appear. These are prone to the deafness associated with odd- or blue-eyed white cats.

Angora

Turkish in origin, this svelte and athletic cat is one of the oldest known longhaired cat breeds. The Angora was brought to Europe in the 16th century, but thoughtless crossbreeding with other types led to the breed dying out for a time. Fortunately, the Angora was preserved in its home country, although by the 19th century it was endangered and kept in the protection of a zoo. Re-established, the Angora now thrives in Britain and the United States as well as in its native Ankara, where it is also still kept as a domestic pet. Angoras are bred in many colors, although pure white is probably the most popular.

Black and White Problem

Deafness is common in blue- or odd-eyed white Angoras. A black tuft on the head at birth, however, indicates that a kitten probably has good hearing in at least one ear.

Soft Touch

The Angora's coat is fairly long, with a slight wave that gives it a very elegant appearance. There is no thick undercoat, but the fur is enticingly silky and sensuous to touch. The coat on the underparts should be long and form a rich ruff on the cat's chest.

CATERISTICS

Shedding makes regular grooming essential

Loyal and quietly spoken, making an intelligent friend

Outstandingly fine and silky fur

READY FOR FUN

You can tell by this cat's alert expression that it loves nothing more than a lively play session. Angoras are not noisy cats, but they do relish a chance to show off their tricks and love an appreciative audience. They adapt well to both town and country life, but their comparative rarity can make them attractive to cat thieves.

GLAMOROUS *Cat*

A guide to the Persian personality, choosing an appropriate name, and reading your cat's character in the stars.

Names and Naming

Choosing a name for your pet is no easy matter. To quote the 19th-century author Samuel Butler: "They say that the test of literary power is whether a man can write an inscription. I say, can he name a kitten? And by this test I am condemned, for I cannot." Here is a selection of names with a Persian slant, to give you some inspiration.

ALEXANDER *After the ancient Macedonian militarist, Alexander the Great, who conquered Persia and many of the surrounding lands in the 3rd century* B.C.

CUPID *The name given to an exquisite cream Persian in the late 19th century, the first-ever recorded pedigree Persian.*

DANDELION *A frivolous name for a cat whose fluffy coat resembles the dandelion seedhead that appears after flowering.*

DEMAVEND *A name for a climbing cat, this is the highest mountain in the Persian cat's homeland.*

FITZGERALD *After Edward Fitzgerald, a man of "quirky but engaging personality," who translated the 12th-century Persian poem "The Rubaiyat of Omar Khayyam."*

HARUN *In memory of Harun Ar-Rashid, the powerful and enigmatic 8th-century Caliph of Baghdad, whose vast territories included the lands of Persia.*

ORMAZD *The Persian god of creation, light, and goodness – a name for a good-as-gold cat.*

PIETRO *The 16th-century traveler Pietro della Valle is credited with introducing the Persian cat into Europe from Asia.*

SCHEHEREZADE *A clever queen who escaped the death that was the usual fate of the king's wives by telling him tales, breaking off at a tantalizing twist in the plot, for one thousand and one nights.*

SINBAD *The intrepid sailor of Persian legend, who had many extraordinary adventures on his travels. A name for a cat with an incurable wanderlust.*

SORAYA *A beautiful woman with bewitching eyes, formerly the Empress of Iran.*

SOUFFLE *A delicate dish as light and airy as a Persian cat's fluffy coat, and requiring just as much care and attention.*

STARLET *For a cat who is glamorous and knows it, and wears her luxurious coat with pride and delight.*

Persian Cat Character

Like all cats, Persians have complex and fascinating personalities. Here are some of their more unusual fads and foibles explained.

Too Much Love

Recently my four-month-old Cream Longhair, Bertie, has started to "kiss" me, purring loudly and sucking at my neck. My skin is starting to look red and blotchy, but when I try to put Bertie down, he gets very upset.

Bertie is treating you as a mother figure, and must become more independent if you are not to have problems. Encourage him to explore outdoors, and ask other members of the family to groom and feed him. Most importantly, prolonged cuddles must be cut down and ended as soon as Bertie shows signs of wanting to "kiss." If he is given stimulation and interest, while remaining certain of your affection, he should soon stop.

TANGLED TROUBLES

Mr. Baxter, my one-year-old Smoke Longhair, cannot stand being groomed. He fights to get away and tries to scratch and bite whenever I come near him with a comb. What should I do?

Enlist someone to help you and stand Mr. Baxter on a surface covered with carpet. Pull him gently backwards, and hold him. He will fix his claws into the carpet, giving you a chance to lightly brush his back: leave more sensitive areas for now. Talk to him softly, and reward him at the end of every session. Gradually, he will allow you to brush him more thoroughly. Ideally, cats should be groomed daily from kittenhood, so that they learn to enjoy it.

OUTDOOR FEAR

Fluffkin used to go out every day, but suddenly she refuses to leave the house, and cries loudly if I put her outside.

Because Fluffkin used to go out, something must have frightened her. Remove or reduce the problem, and you may be able to restore Fluffkin's confidence. Put her out in a carrying basket at first, then a pen where she can still feel safely enclosed. Stay with her until she is more relaxed.

Persian Cat Stars

Your pet's personality, charted in the Zodiac.

Aries

21 MARCH – 20 APRIL

Energetic and adventurous, Arien cats are impatient and demand all your attention.
Arien happiness: Never let them get bored; provide them with a companion.
Arien health: Make sure that they get plenty of exercise. The head can be vulnerable.

Taurus

21 APRIL – 21 MAY

Placid and home-loving, Taurean cats prefer to be the only pet in the household.
Taurean happiness: Make sure that they feel secure; make rules and stick to them.
Taurean health: Prevent overeating. The throat and neck are susceptible to problems.

Gemini

22 MAY – 21 JUNE

Chatty cats, always lively and full of bounce, Geminian felines adapt readily to change.
Geminian happiness: Talk to them, and provide new toys and games frequently.
Geminian health: Watch for problems with nerves; create a calming environment.

Cancer

22 JUNE – 22 JULY

These cats can be almost overwhelmingly devoted to their owners, and are easily hurt. *Cancerian happiness:* Stroke and reassure them, and learn to understand their moods. *Cancerian health:* Avoid rich foods, as the stomach is often delicate and readily upset.

Leo

23 JULY – 23 AUGUST

Leonine cats rule the roost, and other pets soon find out who's head of the household. *Leonine happiness:* Recognize their sensitivity, even when they seem overconfident. *Leonine health:* Don't let them overdo it and exhaust themselves. The back may be weak.

Virgo

24 AUGUST – 22 SEPTEMBER

Shy and retiring, these cats are happiest in the company of those they know and love. *Virgoan happiness:* Encourage them to relax. Keep their surroundings clean and tidy. *Virgoan health:* Make sure that they get fresh air every day. The stomach may give trouble.

Libra

23 SEPTEMBER – 23 OCTOBER

Cats born under Libra are beautiful – and know it! Incurable flirts, they love people. *Libran happiness:* Spoil them with a little luxury. Don't leave them alone too much. *Libran health:* Give rich foods only as a treat. Kidneys are vulnerable to disease.

Scorpio

24 OCTOBER – 22 NOVEMBER

Scorpio cats always get their own way. They love their owners with unrivaled intensity. *Scorpio happiness:* Return their love and show them how much you care. *Scorpio health:* Give them lots to do. Expectant mothers need special attention.

Sagittarius

23 NOVEMBER – 21 DECEMBER

There's no subtlety about this sign, but a carefree love of life that is very endearing. *Sagittarian happiness:* Let them roam freee – they can't stand being confined to the house. *Sagittarian health:* Try to curb their daredevil streak. Hip problems are possible.

Capricorn

22 DECEMBER – 20 JANUARY

Careful Capricornian cats can tiptoe along a shelf of china without breaking a piece. *Capricornian happiness:* Appreciate their loyalty and encourage their affection. *Capricornian health:* Encourage exercise. Teeth and skin are prone to minor ailments.

Aquarius

21 JANUARY – 18 FEBRUARY

Quirky and clever, Aquarian cats tend to keep aloof and value their independence. *Aquarian happiness:* Accept their unconventionality; give them freedom. *Aquarian health:* Remember that they dislike heat and may have poor circulation.

Pisces

19 FEBRUARY – 20 MARCH

Sensitive creatures, Piscean cats are loving in their way, but can be hard to pin down. *Piscean happiness:* Prevent trivial mishaps – their delicate feelings are easily upset. *Piscean health:* Allow for their reaction to the weather. Paws must be well cared for.

PAMPERED *Cat*

A useful compendium of the day-to-day care essential in the keeping of Persian cats

CHOOSING A KITTEN

Picking out the right little bundle of fluff to take home with you can be a hard decision: every single kitten in a litter is so adorable.

HOUSE CAT OR SHOW CAT?

A Persian kitten is ideal if you want a calm, friendly, family cat and you can spare the time for daily grooming. You can simply choose your favorite from any healthy litter. If you want to show your cat, go to a reputable breeder. Kittens are born with blue eyes, and the brilliant orange or copper of some types develop gradually. Coat colors and markings can also alter, so it can be difficult to tell whether a kitten will be suitable for showing when it is older. A breeder can advise you.

LIFE OF LUXURY

Longhairs are justly renowned for their generally easygoing and affectionate natures. Don't be surprised if your new pet wants to spend as much time as possible curled up on your lap.

SWEET DREAMS

Kittens need plenty of sleep to recover from their playtimes. Provide a comfortable bed, but be prepared for kitty to choose a snoozing spot elsewhere.

WHICH KITTEN?

When you make your choice, watch the kittens at play.

1 *Choose a lively kitten with lots of energy.*

2 *Handle the kittens, and choose one that enjoys being picked up and stroked.*

3 *Bright eyes, clean nose and ears, and a silky coat are all signs of good health.*

4 *The teeth should be white, the gums pink and firm, and the breath sweet.*

5 *Check that the kitten can jump and run with ease.*

6 *Consider taking two kittens, to satisfy these cats' incurable love of companionship.*

HELLO...

Make family introductions slowly: it takes time to form lasting friendships.

Cat Glamour

Cats know very well how beautiful they are: they can tell by all the admiring looks and compliments that come their way. Many devote hours to grooming themselves, but a longhaired cat needs a little help from its friends to keep that glorious coat tangle-free. A few minutes grooming each day will help keep your cat looking perfect.

Brush Work

You will need a range of brushes and combs from a pet shop. Take care to keep them scrupulously clean.

Grooming Guide

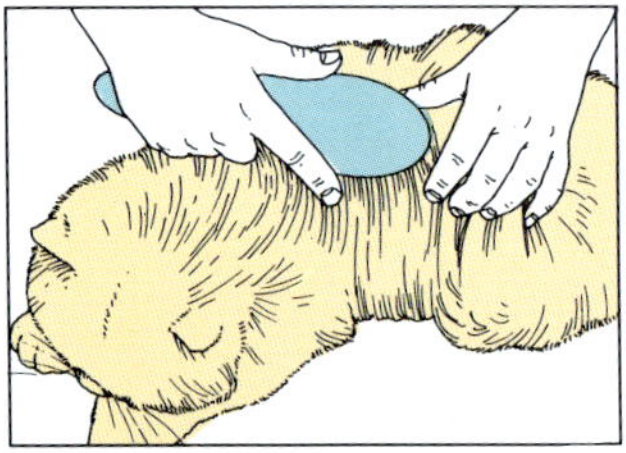

1 *Brush the fur up and away from the body to remove any dead hairs.*

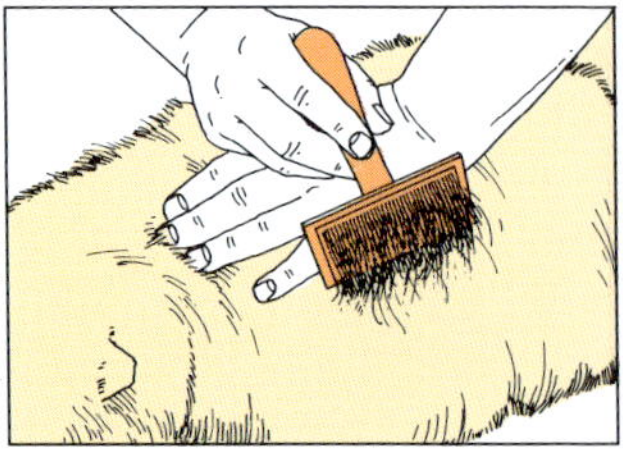

2 *Brush down with a wire slicker brush over the whole body.*

Eye Wise

Gently wipe away tear marks with a cotton ball moistened in slightly salted water. Avoid the eyes themselves.

Pearly Whites

Check teeth and gums regularly. A weekly cleaning will keep the breath sweet and the teeth free of tartar. Prevent plaque from building up on the teeth by brushing with a small-headed toothbrush dipped in pet toothpaste or salt water.

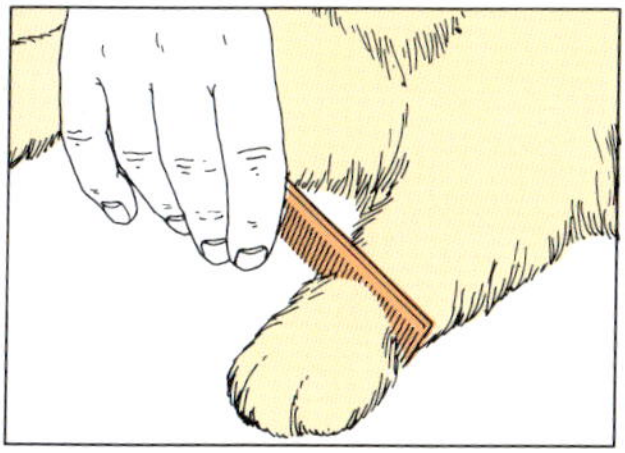

3 *Get to work on any serious tangles with a comb, teasing them out gently.*

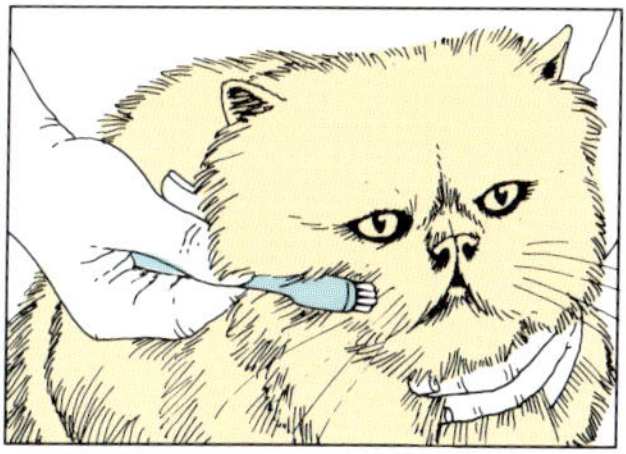

4 *Fluff up the face ruff using a toothbrush – but take care to avoid the eyes.*

Persian Cuisine

Your Persian cat will appreciate specially cooked dishes with a slightly exotic twist. Always allow food to cool before serving it, and make sure that fresh drinking water is readily available.

Chicken Kofta

Finely chop a breast of chicken and a strip of bacon. Soak a slice of white bread in water, squeeze thoroughly, crumble, and add to chicken. Stir in a beaten egg and a tablespoon of chopped parsley, and form into tiny balls. Fry in oil until completely cooked through.

Zucchini Frittata

Wash, peel, and slice a small zucchini, and boil in water until tender. Place slices in a frying pan, pour on two beaten eggs, and cook gently over a very low heat until the eggs are set. Brown top under the grill. Allow the dish to cool completely, chop finely, and serve.

Lamb Kebabs

Alternate small cubes of lamb, kidney, and mushrooms on a skewer. Grill until well cooked. Remove from skewer to serve.

Shrimp Delight

Poach shrimps for five minutes in water flavored with scallions, celery leaves, and lemon juice. Drain well and peel.

Bulgur Pilaf

Cook cracked wheat in boiling water until it is swollen and tender. Braise chopped lamb's liver in stock until cooked through, then combine with the bulgur to serve.

Liver Treat

Finely chop some chicken livers. Fry them gently until they are cooked through but still moist. Add a beaten egg to the pan and continue to cook, stirring, until the egg is set.

Couscous

Steam couscous until tender. Cook a piece of stewing lamb in a pressure cooker, remove bones, and chop finely. Serve moistened with the cooking liquid, with the couscous.

Apple Delectation

A typical Persian dessert. Peel a sweet eating apple and grate the flesh finely. Sprinkle with a little lemon juice and rosewater. Serve in small portions.

My Cat's Personal Record

Name . . . .

Pedigree name . . . .

Date of birth . . . . Sex . . . .

Breed . . . .

Color and markings . . . .

. . . .

Color of eyes . . . .

Name and breed of mother . . . .

. . . .

Name and breed of father . . . .

. . . .

Name and address of breeder . . . .

. . . .

. . . .

Cat show prizes . . . .

. . . .

Favorite foods and drinks ....

....

Best places to stroke ....

....

Sunniest snoozing spot ....

Coziest corner ....

Preferred people ....

....

Vocabulary (list sounds and translations) ....

....

Body language (describe movements and meanings) ....

....

....

....

Attention-grabbing ploys ....

....

Most memorable moments ....

....

A-Z OF PERSIAN CATS

A IS FOR AGGRESSION
Rarely seen in the Persian cat, which is renowned for its peaceable nature.

B IS FOR BATH
Pale-toned and white Persians benefit from a bath before showing. The calmest characters can even be dried with a hairdryer.

C IS FOR CAESAREAN
Becoming more common. Persians may experience difficulty in birthing because of their small hips and large heads.

D IS FOR DOCILE
Like all cats, the Persian does not respond well to being teased, but it is generally famous for its obliging personality.

E IS FOR ELDERLY
Take your senior citizen cat to the vet for a health check-up every three to four months, to catch age-associated problems at an early stage.

F IS FOR FEAR
Cats sometimes develop a fear of men, possibly because male voices are generally loud and deep. Male cat fans should speak softly and handle a frightened cat with extreme care.

G IS FOR GASTRIC UPSETS
Hairballs are often the cause. If commercial hairball medicine doesn't do the trick, consult your vet.

H IS FOR HOUSETRAINING
Persians may find litter habits harder to learn than other breeds. Never punish accidents, and make sure your new kitten is already well trained when you take it home.

I IS FOR INDOOR LIFE

Many Persian cats are destined for a housebound life. Fortunately, most longhaired cats do not object to being confined and are more than content to spend their days in the home.

J IS FOR JUDGING

Show cats are judged on many points particular to their breed, such as eye shape and color, physical build, and the quality of the coat. Their general condition is also taken into account.

K IS FOR KITTENS

Persian kittens are among the most delightful of all baby cats. To avoid struggles with tangles later on in life, get them used to gentle grooming early on, using a small, soft brush.

L IS FOR LEAVING

If you are traveling abroad or cannot take your cat with you, make sure it is looked after in a cattery, by a cat-sitting agency, or by neighbors. Reduce grooming problems by clipping the fur short in the cat's "armpits," on the inner thighs, and beneath the tail. Any other areas especially prone to matting on your cat could also be trimmed down to make the daily brush-up less of a chore for your sitter.

M IS FOR MUZZLE

A drastic but effective remedy for a cat that struggles during grooming. A muzzle that loosely hoods the face helps to calm the cat, who will crouch low and stop moving.

N IS FOR NIGHT CALLING

Older cats may cry for attention during the night, a sign of their growing dependency on their owners. Provide a warm, secure bed and give plenty of love and reassurance during the day.

O IS FOR OBEDIENCE

Always call your cat by name when you are announcing supper, or to bring it in last thing at night. This way your pet learns its name, and will pay proper attention when you are praising or scolding. Be both firm and consistent in what you do and don't allow, and say "No" as if you really mean it when you discover your cat misbehaving.

P IS FOR PEKE-FACE

A newly developed variety of Persian cat, with an exceptionally flat face and snub nose. These characteristics are controversial, because the shape of the face can cause the cat problems such as blocked tear ducts and difficulties with breathing.

Q IS FOR QUEENS

Unneutered queens will try every trick they know to find a mate, and often succeed despite your best efforts. If you want to breed from a queen, you will have to find a suitable suitor and take her to him. Mothers who are usually allowed to roam outside should be confined to the home for the final two weeks of pregnancy, so that the birth can be supervised. The average length of gestation is 65 days.

R IS FOR REGISTRATION

Vital for pedigree kittens, who must be properly registered with the relevant organization before they can be entered for any cat shows. Details of names, colors, and parents must be given.

S IS FOR SAFETY

Beware of open windows, which might tempt a cat on to a narrow ledge; keep all kitchen utensils put away and rule worktops out of bounds; make sure rubber bands and small objects are safely out of reach; and be aware of household products that are poisonous and store them where they won't provide a temptation to lick or nibble.

T IS FOR TANGLES

The importance of thorough daily grooming can't be overemphasized: it's the only way to keep tangles at bay. Once a longhaired cat's fur becomes badly matted or knotted, the only solution may be dramatic clipping, which will leave your pet looking rather odd.

U is for Understanding

Don't underestimate your Persian cat's intelligence: these fluffy felines may be quiet and gentle, but they are by no means stupid.

V is for Vaccinations

Vital for your cat's continued health, and essential if you plan to show or board your pet. First shots are due at 12 weeks of age, with annual boosters.

W is for Wetting

Persians can be fastidious creatures, and may refuse to use damp litter, preferring a nice dry floor instead. Remove soiled patches of litter frequently, and give the whole tray a thorough cleaning twice a week.

X is for Xquisite

The dictionary definition of this word is "extremely beautiful . . . sensitive . . . of unusual delicacy . . . fastidious . . . refined" – and it fits a Persian perfectly.

Y is for Yawning

This is seen by cats as a reassuring gesture. If you have trouble soothing a particularly anxious cat, try looking at it and giving a wide yawn: the cat may even respond by yawning back at you in imitation.

Z is for Zoroastrism

A religion as venerable as the Persian cat itself, Zoroastrism, like the cat, also has its origins in the Middle East. Its founder, Zoroaster, was an ancient prophet who would exhort his followers to perform good deeds in order to assist the supreme god Ahura Mazda in his eternal struggle against the evil spirit Ahriman.

INDEX

Acknowledgments

Key: t=top; b=bottom; c=center; l=left; r=right

DK Pictures

Steve Gorton and Tim Ridley: 16 cr, 26, 29 t, 41, 49, 50-51, 54-55, 57
Marc Henrie: 7, 8, 9, 16cl, bl, 17bl, 18l, c, cr, br, 19tl, tc, tr, bl, bc, 21t, 22-23b, 24, 25t, 29b, 31b, 32-33, 34-35, 36, 39, 40, 59
Dave King: 5, 14-15, 16br, 17 tl, tr, cl, cr, 19 cl, c, cr, br, 20, 21 b, 22, 25b, 27, 28, 30, 31 t, 37, 40-41 b, 46, 47, 48, 56
Matthew Ward: 17 br, 23 tr

Agency Pictures

Bridgeman Art Library: 11b, 13b
E.T. Archive: 10
Robert Harding: 11t
Roger-Viollet: 12, 13t

Design Assistance: *Patrizio Semproni*
Picture Research: *Diana Morris*
Illustration: *Susan Robertson, Stephen Lings, Clive Spong*